From Idea to Impact
A Guide to Launching Sustainable Start-ups

JJ Johnson

The first edition was published in 2023

ISBN:
Published by:
Sunshine
1663 Liberty Drive
Hyderabad, IN 47403
www.Sunshinepublishers.com

This book is self-published using on-demand printing and publishing, which allows it to be printed and distributed globally.

TABLE OF CONTENTS

Chapter 1: Introduction to Sustainable Start-ups

Defining Sustainable Start-ups

In today's rapidly evolving business landscape, the concept of sustainability has gained significant traction among entrepreneurs and start-ups. As society becomes increasingly aware of the urgent need to address environmental, social, and economic challenges, sustainable start-ups have emerged as a powerful force for positive change. This subchapter aims to provide a comprehensive understanding of what defines a sustainable start-up and why it matters.

First and foremost, a sustainable start-up can be defined as a venture that operates with a clear commitment to minimizing its negative impact on the environment while maximizing its positive social and economic contributions. Unlike traditional start-ups that solely focus on generating profits, sustainable start-ups adopt a triple-bottom-line approach, considering people, planet, and profit.

One key aspect of sustainable start-ups is their dedication to environmental sustainability. These ventures actively seek ways to reduce their carbon footprint, conserve resources, and adopt environmentally friendly practices throughout their value chain. They may embrace renewable energy sources, implement waste reduction strategies, or use sustainable materials in their products or services. By prioritizing sustainability, these start-ups contribute to the larger goal of mitigating climate change and preserving our planet for future generations.

Moreover, sustainable start-ups also prioritize social impact. They recognize the importance of fostering positive relationships with employees, customers, communities, and other stakeholders. These ventures often prioritize fair labor practices, diversity and inclusion, and ethical sourcing. By focusing on social sustainability, sustainable start-ups contribute to creating a more equitable and just society.

Lastly, sustainable start-ups aim to achieve long-term financial viability while also making a positive impact. They understand that financial success is crucial for sustainability and growth. By integrating sustainable practices into their business models, these ventures aim to create value for their investors while addressing pressing societal challenges.

For entrepreneurs diving into the start-up world, embracing sustainability is not only a moral imperative but also a strategic advantage. Consumers and investors are increasingly seeking out sustainable solutions, recognizing the long-term benefits they provide. By aligning their business with sustainability principles, start-ups can differentiate themselves in the market, attract a loyal customer base, and secure investment opportunities.

In conclusion, sustainable start-ups are ventures that prioritize environmental, social, and economic sustainability. These ventures operate with a triple-bottom-line approach, balancing people, planet, and profit. By minimizing their environmental impact, fostering social responsibility, and pursuing financial viability, sustainable start-ups have the potential to drive positive change and contribute to a more sustainable future. As an entrepreneur, embracing sustainability in your start-up not only aligns with societal values but also positions your venture for long-term success and impact.

The Importance of Sustainable Start-ups

In today's rapidly changing world, the concept of sustainability has gained immense significance. As entrepreneurs, it is crucial for us to recognize the importance of integrating sustainability into our start-ups. This subchapter will delve into the reasons why sustainable start-ups are not just a trend, but a necessity for our businesses and for the planet.

First and foremost, sustainable start-ups have the power to create a positive impact on the environment. By incorporating eco-friendly practices, such as using renewable energy sources and reducing waste, we can significantly reduce our carbon footprint. This not only helps combat climate change but also appeals to an increasingly conscious consumer base. Consumers are now actively seeking products and services that align with their values, and sustainable start-ups have a competitive advantage in meeting these demands.

Furthermore, sustainable start-ups have the potential to drive innovation. By prioritizing sustainability, we are forced to think outside the box and develop creative solutions to complex problems. This leads to the development of new technologies, business models, and practices that contribute to a more sustainable future. By being at the forefront of sustainable innovation, we can attract investors, collaborators, and customers who are interested in supporting companies that are making a real difference.

In addition to environmental and innovation benefits, sustainable start-ups also have economic advantages. By focusing on sustainability, we can reduce costs through energy and resource efficiency. This allows us to save money in the long run and increase our profitability. Sustainable practices also foster long-term business resilience by ensuring a reliable supply chain and reducing risks associated with environmental regulations.

Lastly, committing to sustainability can enhance our brand reputation and attract top talent. In today's competitive start-up landscape, having a strong and ethical brand is crucial for success. By embodying sustainability values, we can build trust with our customers, investors, and employees, creating a loyal and engaged community around our brand.

In conclusion, sustainable start-ups are not just an ethical choice but a strategic one. By integrating sustainability into our business models, we can create a positive impact on the environment, drive innovation, reduce costs, enhance our brand reputation, and attract top talent. As entrepreneurs, it is our responsibility to launch start-ups that contribute to a more sustainable and prosperous future for all.

The Role of Entrepreneurs in Driving Sustainability

As entrepreneurs in the startup world, you possess a unique power to drive sustainability and make a positive impact on our planet. In this subchapter, we will explore the crucial role that entrepreneurs play in creating sustainable businesses and the steps you can take to integrate sustainability into your ventures.

At its core, sustainability is about meeting the needs of the present without compromising the ability of future generations to meet their own needs. As entrepreneurs, you have the opportunity to develop innovative solutions that not only address societal and environmental challenges but also generate economic value. By incorporating sustainability into your business model, you can create a win-win situation that benefits both your bottom line and the planet.

First and foremost, it is essential to recognize that sustainability goes beyond simply implementing eco-friendly practices. While reducing waste, conserving resources, and minimizing carbon emissions are crucial, true sustainability encompasses a broader perspective. It involves considering the social, economic, and environmental impacts of your business throughout its entire lifecycle.

One way entrepreneurs can drive sustainability is by embedding it into their company's purpose and values. By aligning your business goals with sustainable development objectives, you can attract like-minded employees, investors, and customers who are committed to making a positive change. Embracing sustainability as a core principle will not only differentiate your startup but also provide a strong foundation for long-term success.

Furthermore, entrepreneurs can leverage innovation and technology to develop sustainable solutions. Through research and development, you can create products or services that not only address pressing environmental issues but also provide superior performance and value to customers. By focusing on sustainability, you can tap into new markets, attract eco-conscious consumers, and gain a competitive edge.

Collaboration is another key aspect of driving sustainability as entrepreneurs. By partnering with other organizations, government bodies, and non-profit entities, you can amplify your impact and tackle complex challenges together. Collaborative efforts can lead to knowledge sharing, resource optimization, and the development of collective solutions that benefit society as a whole.

In conclusion, entrepreneurs have a vital role to play in driving sustainability. By integrating sustainability into your startup's purpose, values, and practices, you can create a positive impact on both the environment and society. Embrace sustainability not only as a tool for differentiation but also as a means to unlock new opportunities and drive long-term success. Together, let's build businesses that not only thrive economically but also contribute to a more sustainable and equitable future.

Chapter 2: Identifying a Sustainable Business Idea

Understanding Market Trends and Needs

In the fast-paced and ever-evolving world of entrepreneurship and start-ups, it is crucial for aspiring entrepreneurs to have a deep understanding of market trends and needs. This subchapter will delve into the importance of comprehending market dynamics and provide valuable insights on how to identify and capitalize on emerging trends.

Market trends are the driving forces behind consumer behavior and purchasing decisions. As an entrepreneur, it is essential to stay up-to-date with the latest trends in your industry to remain relevant and competitive. By understanding these trends, you can predict future customer needs and adapt your products or services accordingly.

One of the first steps in understanding market trends is conducting thorough market research. This involves analyzing data, identifying target markets, and assessing consumer preferences and demands. By doing so, entrepreneurs can gain invaluable insights into what their potential customers are looking for and tailor their offerings to meet those needs.

Furthermore, market trends not only provide entrepreneurs with a competitive edge but also offer potential opportunities for innovation and disruption. By recognizing emerging trends, entrepreneurs can develop groundbreaking ideas and create products or services that fill gaps in the market. This proactive approach can lead to a first-mover advantage and establish a strong market presence.

Another aspect of understanding market trends is keeping a close eye on technological advancements. Technological innovations often shape market trends and consumer behaviors. By embracing emerging technologies and incorporating them into their business strategies, entrepreneurs can position themselves as pioneers in their respective industries.

Moreover, entrepreneurs should also consider the social, economic, and environmental factors that influence market trends. Being mindful of sustainability and ethical practices can enhance the overall appeal of a start-up and attract socially conscious consumers.

In conclusion, understanding market trends and needs is paramount for entrepreneurs looking to launch sustainable start-ups. By conducting thorough market research, staying abreast of industry developments, and embracing technological advancements, entrepreneurs can position themselves as key players in their industries. By capitalizing on emerging trends, entrepreneurs can not only meet customer needs effectively but also innovate and disrupt markets, leading to a successful and impactful start-up journey.

Assessing Environmental and Social Impact Opportunities

In today's rapidly changing business landscape, entrepreneurs and start-ups have a unique opportunity to make a positive impact on the world. The growing awareness of environmental and social issues has created a demand for sustainable solutions, and consumers are increasingly looking to support businesses that align with their values. This subchapter delves into the importance of assessing environmental and social impact opportunities, providing invaluable insights for entrepreneurs looking to launch sustainable start-ups.

One of the first steps in assessing environmental and social impact opportunities is conducting a thorough analysis of the current landscape. This includes researching and understanding the pressing environmental and social challenges that exist in your target market. By identifying these challenges, you can uncover potential opportunities to develop innovative solutions that address these issues effectively.

Furthermore, it is essential to evaluate the feasibility and scalability of your proposed solutions. Entrepreneurs need to consider the potential impact their start-up can have and how it can be scaled up to reach a larger audience. This involves assessing the market demand, the availability of necessary resources, and the potential for growth and expansion.

In addition to the feasibility assessment, entrepreneurs should also consider the potential risks and challenges associated with their environmental and social impact initiatives. Identifying and addressing these risks proactively can help avoid potential pitfalls and ensure the long-term sustainability of the start-up.

Collaboration and partnerships play a crucial role in maximizing environmental and social impact opportunities. Entrepreneurs should explore opportunities to collaborate with like-minded organizations, non-profits, and government agencies to leverage their expertise and resources. Collaborative efforts can amplify the impact of start-ups and create a more significant positive change.

Finally, entrepreneurs need to measure and track the impact of their initiatives continuously. Establishing key performance indicators (KPIs) allows start-ups to assess the effectiveness of their solutions and make necessary adjustments to maximize impact. Regular impact assessments enable entrepreneurs to demonstrate the tangible benefits of their start-ups to potential investors, customers, and other stakeholders.

In conclusion, assessing environmental and social impact opportunities is a crucial step for entrepreneurs aiming to launch sustainable start-ups. By conducting a comprehensive analysis, evaluating feasibility, addressing risks, fostering collaboration, and measuring impact, entrepreneurs can pave the way for a successful and impactful venture. By combining business acumen with a focus on environmental and social sustainability, entrepreneurs can create a brighter and more sustainable future for both their start-ups and the world at large.

Leveraging Technology for Sustainable Solutions

In this rapidly evolving digital era, entrepreneurs have a unique opportunity to leverage technology for the greater good and create sustainable solutions. Technology has the potential to transform the way we address the pressing environmental and social challenges of our time, and startups are at the forefront of this revolution.

The power of technology lies in its ability to scale solutions and reach a global audience. Startups can harness this power to develop innovative products and services that not only address sustainability issues but also create a positive impact on society. By combining technology with sustainability, entrepreneurs can drive change and build profitable businesses that contribute to a more sustainable future.

One area where technology can make a significant impact is energy. Startups can develop smart grids, energy-efficient systems, and renewable energy solutions that reduce carbon emissions and reliance on fossil fuels. By leveraging technology such as artificial intelligence (AI) and the Internet of Things (IoT), entrepreneurs can optimize energy consumption, monitor energy usage, and enable energy storage, leading to a more sustainable and efficient energy infrastructure.

Another area where technology can drive sustainable solutions is agriculture. With a growing global population, it is crucial to find ways to produce food in a more sustainable and efficient manner. Startups can develop precision farming techniques that utilize sensors, drones, and AI to monitor crop health, optimize irrigation, and reduce the use of harmful pesticides. By leveraging technology, entrepreneurs can help create a more sustainable and resilient food system.

Furthermore, technology can play a vital role in waste management and recycling. Startups can develop innovative waste management solutions that use AI and machine learning to identify recycling opportunities and reduce the amount of waste sent to landfills. By leveraging technology, entrepreneurs can contribute to the circular economy by turning waste into valuable resources, reducing environmental pollution, and promoting sustainable consumption patterns.

In conclusion, technology presents entrepreneurs with a unique opportunity to create sustainable solutions and launch successful startups. By leveraging technology in areas such as energy, agriculture, and waste management, entrepreneurs can address pressing sustainability challenges and make a positive impact on society and the environment. As entrepreneurs, it is our responsibility to embrace technology and utilize it as a powerful tool for driving sustainable change.

Chapter 3: Conducting Market Research for Sustainable Start-ups

Defining Target Market Segments

One of the key elements in launching a successful start-up is understanding your target market segments. Identifying and defining these segments is crucial for entrepreneurs looking to create sustainable businesses. In this subchapter, we will explore the importance of defining target market segments and how it can help you maximize the impact of your start-up.

When starting a business, many entrepreneurs make the mistake of trying to target a broad audience. They believe that by appealing to as many people as possible, they will increase their chances of success. However, taking a more focused approach by defining target market segments can actually lead to greater success.

Defining target market segments involves breaking down your potential customers into specific groups based on demographics, psychographics, behaviors, and other relevant factors. By doing so, you gain a deeper understanding of your customers' needs, preferences, and pain points, allowing you to tailor your product or service to meet their specific requirements.

Understanding your target market segments also helps you identify the most profitable customer groups. By focusing your resources on those segments that are most likely to buy from you, you can optimize your marketing efforts and increase your chances of generating revenue. This targeted approach allows you to allocate your limited resources effectively, saving both time and money.

Moreover, defining target market segments enables you to differentiate your start-up from competitors. By understanding the unique characteristics and preferences of your customer segments, you can position your offering in a way that stands out in the market. This differentiation can be a key driver of success, as it creates a compelling value proposition that attracts customers and builds brand loyalty.

To define your target market segments, start by conducting market research. Use surveys, interviews, and other methods to gather data on your potential customers' demographics, interests, behaviors, and pain points. Analyze this information to identify commonalities and patterns, which will help you group your customers into segments.

Once you have defined your target market segments, develop detailed buyer personas for each group. These personas should include information such as age, gender, occupation, interests, and purchasing behavior. Having a clear understanding of these personas will guide your marketing and sales strategies and enable you to create targeted messaging and campaigns.

In conclusion, defining target market segments is a critical step for entrepreneurs launching sustainable start-ups. By understanding your customers' needs and preferences, focusing your resources on profitable segments, and differentiating your offering, you can maximize the impact of your business and increase your chances of success in the competitive start-up landscape.

Analyzing Competitors and Industry Landscape

In the fast-paced world of entrepreneurship and start-ups, understanding your competitors and the industry landscape is crucial for success. The ability to analyze and gain insights into the market can provide you with a competitive advantage, helping you make informed decisions and differentiate your start-up from others. This subchapter will guide you through the process of analyzing competitors and the industry landscape, equipping you with the tools and knowledge necessary to thrive in your chosen niche.

Competitor analysis forms the foundation of a solid business strategy. By identifying and assessing your direct and indirect competitors, you can gain insights into their strengths, weaknesses, and market positioning. This analysis allows you to identify opportunities and threats within the industry, enabling you to refine your business model and differentiate your product or service. Through various techniques such as SWOT analysis, market research, and customer feedback, you can gather valuable data that will inform your decision-making process.

Furthermore, understanding the broader industry landscape is essential for identifying trends, market gaps, and potential disruptors. By conducting a thorough analysis, you can uncover emerging technologies, changing consumer preferences, and regulatory factors that may impact your start-up. This knowledge allows you to adapt and innovate, ensuring your business remains relevant and resilient in a dynamic market.

To effectively analyze competitors and the industry landscape, you must utilize a combination of primary and secondary research methods. Primary research involves directly interacting with customers, conducting surveys, and engaging in focus groups to gather insights. Secondary research involves analyzing existing data, reports, and industry publications. By utilizing both approaches, you can obtain a comprehensive understanding of your market, customers, and competition.

In this subchapter, we will delve into the various tools and techniques that can be used for competitor and industry analysis. We will explore frameworks such as Porter's Five Forces, PESTEL analysis, and the Value Chain, providing you with practical guidance on how to apply these models to your start-up. Additionally, we will discuss the importance of continuous monitoring and adapting your analysis as the market evolves.

Analyzing competitors and the industry landscape is an ongoing process. By embracing this mindset and regularly updating your insights, you can position your start-up for long-term success. The knowledge gained through this analysis will not only inform your strategic decisions but also enable you to identify opportunities for collaboration, partnerships, and market expansion. With a deep understanding of your competitors and industry, you can navigate the start-up ecosystem with confidence, maximizing your chances of achieving sustainable growth and impact.

Identifying Market Gaps and Opportunities

Introduction:

In the ever-evolving world of entrepreneurship, the ability to identify market gaps and opportunities is crucial for the success of any startup. This subchapter aims to guide entrepreneurs through the process of recognizing untapped market potential and leveraging it to create sustainable and impactful businesses. By understanding the significance of market gaps and opportunities, entrepreneurs can strategically position their startups for long-term success.

Understanding Market Gaps: A market gap refers to an unmet or underserved customer need within a specific industry or market segment. Identifying these gaps requires a deep understanding of customer pain points, desires, and existing solutions. Entrepreneurs must conduct thorough market research, analyze consumer behavior, and engage in competitive analysis to identify these gaps accurately. By doing so, they can uncover opportunities to develop innovative products or services that cater to unmet needs.

Leveraging Market Opportunities: Market opportunities arise from various factors such as technological advancements, changing consumer preferences, or emerging trends. Entrepreneurs need to stay informed about these developments to capitalize on potential opportunities. Researching industry trends, attending conferences, and networking with experts in the field can provide valuable insights into emerging markets or gaps that can be exploited. By leveraging market opportunities, startups can gain a competitive advantage and position themselves as industry leaders.

Validation and Testing: Identifying market gaps and opportunities is only the first step. Entrepreneurs need to validate their assumptions and test their ideas before launching a startup. Conducting market surveys, focus groups, or even developing a minimum viable product (MVP) can help gather feedback and refine the business concept. This iterative approach allows startups to adapt their offerings to meet customer needs effectively.

Strategic Planning: Once a market gap or opportunity has been identified and validated, entrepreneurs must develop a strategic plan to address it. This includes defining the target market, crafting a unique value proposition, and outlining a business model that aligns with the identified gap. Entrepreneurs should also assess potential risks, competitors, and scalability factors to ensure long-term sustainability.

Conclusion:

Identifying market gaps and opportunities is a fundamental aspect of launching sustainable startups. By understanding customer needs, staying informed about emerging trends, validating assumptions, and developing strategic plans, entrepreneurs can position their startups for success. This subchapter provides valuable insights and actionable steps for entrepreneurs to identify and leverage market gaps and opportunities, ultimately leading to impactful and sustainable businesses.

Chapter 4: Developing a Sustainable Business Model

Choosing the Right Legal Structure

When embarking on your entrepreneurial journey, one of the most critical decisions you will face is choosing the right legal structure for your startup. The legal structure you select will have implications for your business's financial, operational, and legal aspects. Therefore, it is essential to thoroughly understand your options and choose wisely. This subchapter will provide you with a comprehensive guide to help you navigate this important decision-making process.

There are several legal structures you can consider for your startup, including sole proprietorship, partnership, limited liability company (LLC), and corporation. Each structure has its own advantages and disadvantages, so it is crucial to evaluate them based on your specific needs and goals.

Sole proprietorship is the simplest legal structure, suitable for solo entrepreneurs. It offers complete control over your business but also leaves you personally liable for any debts or legal issues. Partnerships, on the other hand, allow you to share responsibilities and resources with one or more individuals. However, it is crucial to have a solid partnership agreement in place to avoid potential conflicts and ensure a smooth operation.

LLCs combine the benefits of partnerships and corporations. They provide limited liability protection for owners while maintaining flexibility in management and taxation. LLCs are popular among startups due to their simplicity and protection for personal assets. Alternatively, corporations offer the most robust liability protection, but they require more formalities and compliance, such as holding regular shareholder meetings and keeping detailed records.

To choose the right legal structure, consider factors like liability protection, tax implications, management structure, and funding options. Additionally, assess your long-term goals and the potential growth trajectory of your startup. If you plan to seek external investment or go public in the future, a corporate structure may be more suitable.

It is highly recommended to consult with legal and financial professionals who specialize in startup law to ensure you make an informed decision. They can provide personalized advice based on your unique circumstances and help you navigate the legal complexities.

Remember, choosing the right legal structure is a crucial step in setting up a sustainable startup. Take the time to thoroughly research and evaluate your options to ensure your business is built on a solid foundation. By making the right choice, you can protect your personal assets, optimize tax benefits, and position your startup for long-term success.

Incorporating Environmental and Social Objectives

In today's rapidly changing business landscape, entrepreneurs and start-ups have a unique opportunity to not only create successful and profitable ventures but also make a positive impact on the environment and society. Incorporating environmental and social objectives into your start-up's core values is not only a responsible choice but also a strategic one. Consumers are increasingly conscious of the impact their purchases have on the planet and on communities, and they are actively seeking out businesses that align with their values. By incorporating environmental and social objectives, you can attract a growing market of socially conscious consumers and differentiate your start-up from the competition.

One way to incorporate environmental objectives into your start-up is by adopting sustainable practices throughout your operations. This could include using renewable energy sources, reducing waste, and implementing recycling programs. Emphasize the importance of sustainability in your marketing and communications to show your audience that you are committed to minimizing your ecological footprint.

Social objectives can be incorporated by supporting local communities, fostering diversity and inclusion, and promoting fair labor practices. Consider partnering with local non-profit organizations or donating a portion of your profits to support causes that align with your start-up's values. By doing so, you can build a positive brand image and create a lasting impact on the communities you serve.

Incorporating environmental and social objectives is not without its challenges. Start-ups often face resource constraints and tight budgets, making it difficult to prioritize sustainability initiatives. However, by taking small steps and gradually integrating these objectives into your business model, you can make a meaningful impact over time. Seek out partnerships with like-minded organizations and leverage their expertise and resources to overcome these challenges.

Remember, incorporating environmental and social objectives is not just a trend or marketing ploy. It is a fundamental shift in the way businesses operate. By aligning your start-up with these objectives, you not only contribute to a more sustainable future but also attract a loyal customer base and gain a competitive advantage in the market. The key is to be authentic and transparent in your efforts, engaging with your audience and stakeholders to build trust and credibility.

In conclusion, as an entrepreneur in the start-up niche, incorporating environmental and social objectives into your business model is not only a responsible choice but also a strategic one. By adopting sustainable practices and supporting social causes, you can attract socially conscious consumers, differentiate your start-up, and build a positive brand image. Despite the challenges, taking small steps and leveraging partnerships can help you make a meaningful impact while creating a successful and sustainable business. Embrace this opportunity to make a difference and launch a start-up that not only achieves financial success but also contributes to a better world.

Creating a Value Proposition for Sustainability

In today's fast-paced and ever-changing business landscape, sustainability has emerged as a key driver of success and a crucial consideration for entrepreneurs looking to launch sustainable start-ups. As entrepreneurs, it is imperative to understand the importance of creating a value proposition that revolves around sustainability. This subchapter will delve into the essential elements of developing a value proposition for sustainability and how it can impact your start-up's success.

A value proposition for sustainability encompasses the unique benefits and advantages your start-up offers to customers, society, and the environment. It goes beyond traditional commercial value propositions by integrating social and environmental considerations into your business model. By aligning your start-up's mission with sustainability, you can attract like-minded customers, investors, and partners who share your vision for a better future.

The first step in creating a value proposition for sustainability is to clearly define your start-up's purpose and values. What is the driving force behind your venture? How does it contribute to a more sustainable world? By answering these questions, you can articulate your start-up's unique selling points and differentiate it from competitors.

Next, it is essential to identify your target audience and their sustainability needs. Understanding the preferences and values of your target market will allow you to tailor your value proposition accordingly. For instance, if your start-up offers eco-friendly products, emphasize their low carbon footprint and sustainable sourcing to resonate with environmentally-conscious consumers.

Furthermore, incorporating sustainability metrics and impact assessments into your value proposition can provide credibility and transparency to your stakeholders. By quantifying and showcasing the positive social and environmental outcomes of your start-up, you can attract investors and customers who prioritize sustainability.

Collaboration is another crucial aspect of creating a value proposition for sustainability. Seek partnerships with other sustainable start-ups, NGOs, and government entities to amplify your impact and expand your network. By leveraging collective resources and expertise, you can create innovative solutions to address society's most pressing challenges.

Lastly, continuously monitor and evaluate your value proposition to ensure its relevance and effectiveness. As the sustainable start-up landscape evolves, so should your value proposition. Stay updated on the latest sustainability trends and consumer preferences to remain competitive.

In conclusion, creating a value proposition for sustainability is vital for entrepreneurs launching sustainable start-ups. By aligning your start-up's purpose with sustainable practices, understanding your target audience's needs, quantifying your impact, fostering collaboration, and staying adaptable, you can develop a compelling value proposition that attracts customers and investors passionate about building a more sustainable future. Embrace sustainability as a core element of your start-up's DNA, and you will set yourself apart in the competitive start-up ecosystem.

Chapter 5: Building a Sustainable Start-up Team

Identifying Key Roles and Responsibilities

In the fast-paced world of start-ups, success hinges on having a well-structured and efficient team. As an entrepreneur, you may have a brilliant idea, but it takes a collective effort to turn that idea into a sustainable business. This subchapter will guide you through the process of identifying key roles and responsibilities within your start-up, ensuring that everyone is aligned and working towards a common goal.

One of the first steps in building a successful team is understanding the specific roles and responsibilities needed to drive your start-up forward. While every start-up is unique, there are some key positions that are crucial across various industries. These may include a visionary founder, a skilled technical expert, a marketing guru, a financial strategist, and an operations manager. However, the roles you need will ultimately depend on your business model, goals, and niche.

Once you have a clear idea of the key roles needed, it is important to assess the skills and expertise required for each position. Consider the qualifications, experience, and personality traits that best align with the role. It is also vital to define the responsibilities and tasks associated with each position, ensuring there is no overlap or confusion. This clarity will help you avoid any potential conflicts or gaps in your team's functioning.

While it is essential to find individuals who possess the necessary skills, building a cohesive team goes beyond that. Cultural fit is equally important, as it determines how well your team members collaborate and communicate with each other. Look for individuals who share your values, work ethic, and passion for your start-up's mission. This will create a positive and productive working environment, fostering innovation and creativity.

Once you have identified key roles and responsibilities and found the right individuals to fill those positions, it is crucial to establish clear lines of communication and accountability. Regular team meetings, progress reports, and performance evaluations will help ensure that everyone is on the same page and working towards the same objectives. Encourage open and honest communication, allowing team members to voice their ideas, concerns, and suggestions.

In conclusion, identifying key roles and responsibilities within your start-up is a critical step towards success. By carefully assessing the skills and qualifications required for each position, finding individuals who fit your culture, and establishing effective communication channels, you will build a strong and efficient team. Remember, your team is the backbone of your start-up, and investing time and effort into its formation will lay the foundation for long-term growth and impact.

Attracting and Retaining Mission-Driven Talent

In the fast-paced world of startups, attracting and retaining top talent can make all the difference between success and failure. As an entrepreneur with a mission-driven startup, it is crucial to build a team that is not only skilled and dedicated but also shares your vision and passion. This subchapter will explore strategies and best practices for attracting and retaining mission-driven talent, ensuring that your startup thrives in the long run.

One key aspect of attracting mission-driven talent is clearly articulating your startup's mission and values. It is important to communicate your purpose and the positive impact your startup aims to make in the world. This will help you attract individuals who are aligned with your mission and genuinely passionate about the work they will be doing. Consider incorporating your mission and values into your job postings and interviews to attract like-minded candidates.

In addition to showcasing your mission, offering competitive compensation packages can also play a significant role in attracting top talent. While mission-driven individuals may prioritize purpose over pay, it is essential to offer fair compensation that reflects the skills and experience of your team members. Consider creating a comprehensive benefits package that includes perks like flexible work hours, professional development opportunities, and equity options to entice mission-driven professionals.

Once you have attracted talented individuals to your startup, it is equally important to retain them. Building a strong company culture that aligns with your mission and values can foster a sense of belonging and purpose among your team members. Encourage open communication, collaboration, and a supportive work environment to keep your employees engaged and motivated.

Investing in employee development and growth opportunities is another effective strategy for retaining mission-driven talent. Provide ongoing training, mentorship programs, and opportunities for advancement within your startup. This will not only enhance the skills of your team members but also show them that you are dedicated to their personal and professional growth.

Lastly, never underestimate the power of recognition and appreciation. Celebrate the achievements and contributions of your mission-driven team members regularly. Whether through public recognition, employee awards, or team-building activities, acknowledging their efforts can go a long way in building loyalty and a sense of purpose within your startup.

In conclusion, attracting and retaining mission-driven talent is crucial for the success of your startup. By clearly communicating your mission, offering competitive compensation packages, fostering a strong company culture, investing in employee development, and recognizing their contributions, you can build a team that is passionate, dedicated, and aligned with your startup's long-term goals.

Fostering a Culture of Sustainability and Innovation

In today's rapidly evolving business landscape, sustainability and innovation have become crucial elements for the long-term success of startups. As entrepreneurs, it is essential to understand the importance of fostering a culture that embraces both sustainability and innovation. This subchapter aims to provide valuable insights and practical guidance on how to create an environment that nurtures these critical aspects within your startup.

Sustainability lies at the heart of any successful startup aiming to make a positive impact on society and the environment. It involves considering the long-term consequences of your business decisions, including resource consumption, waste management, and social responsibility. By integrating sustainability practices into your startup's core values, you not only contribute to a greener future but also attract environmentally conscious customers and investors.

To cultivate a culture of sustainability, start by identifying your startup's environmental impact and setting clear sustainability goals. Encourage your team to brainstorm innovative solutions to reduce carbon emissions, minimize waste, and adopt eco-friendly practices. Implementing recycling programs, using renewable energy sources, and promoting telecommuting are just a few examples of sustainable initiatives that can be easily integrated into your startup's operations.

Innovation, on the other hand, is the driving force behind growth and competitiveness in the startup world. It involves constantly challenging the status quo and seeking new ways to solve problems. By creating an environment that fosters innovation, you empower your team to think creatively and develop groundbreaking ideas that can disrupt industries and fuel your startup's growth.

To foster a culture of innovation, encourage open communication and collaboration within your startup. Provide your team with the freedom to experiment, take risks, and learn from failures. Celebrate and reward innovative thinking, and create channels for employees to share their ideas and suggestions. Additionally, invest in continuous learning and development programs to keep your team updated with the latest industry trends and emerging technologies.

The intersection of sustainability and innovation can lead to groundbreaking solutions that not only benefit your startup but also contribute to a better world. By fostering a culture that embraces both, you position your startup as a pioneer in sustainability-driven innovation, attracting like-minded customers and investors who prioritize ethical and environmentally friendly business practices.

In conclusion, cultivating a culture of sustainability and innovation is vital for the success of startups. By integrating sustainability practices into your startup's core values and fostering an environment that encourages innovative thinking, you create a competitive advantage while making a positive impact on the world. Embrace sustainability and innovation as guiding principles, and your startup will be well-positioned for long-term success in today's dynamic business landscape.

Chapter 6: Securing Funding for Sustainable Start-ups

Exploring Funding Options for Sustainable Ventures

In the ever-evolving landscape of entrepreneurship, securing funding for your sustainable start-up is a critical step towards turning your innovative idea into a successful venture. This subchapter aims to guide entrepreneurs in understanding and exploring various funding options available for sustainable ventures.

1.   Bootstrapping:
Bootstrapping refers to financing your start-up using personal savings, credit cards, or funds from family and friends. While it may involve limitations in terms of available capital, it offers the advantage of maintaining complete control over your business and avoiding the debt burden.

2.   Grants   and   Competitions:
Numerous organizations, government agencies, and foundations offer grants and funding opportunities specifically designed for sustainable ventures. These grants not only provide financial support but also offer networking opportunities and exposure to potential investors.

3.   Angel   Investors:
Angel investors are high-net-worth individuals who invest their personal funds into early-stage start-ups. These investors often have a keen interest in sustainable ventures and can provide both

capital and valuable expertise. Connecting with angel investor networks and attending pitch events can increase your chances of securing funding.

4.   Venture   Capital: Venture capital firms invest in start-ups with high-growth potential. While they may be more focused on financial returns, many venture capital firms are increasingly interested in sustainable ventures. Prioritize identifying venture capitalists with a specific focus on sustainability to increase your chances of finding a suitable partner.

5.   Crowdfunding: Crowdfunding platforms have gained popularity in recent years as a means to raise capital from a large number of individuals. By offering rewards or equity, entrepreneurs can attract backers who believe in their sustainable vision. Utilizing social media and running a compelling campaign can significantly boost your crowdfunding efforts.

6.   Impact   Investors: Impact investors prioritize both financial returns and positive social and environmental impact. They often provide patient capital and long-term support to sustainable ventures. Engaging with impact investment networks and demonstrating your venture's potential for positive change can attract this type of funding.

7.   Strategic   Partnerships: Forming strategic partnerships with existing companies or

organizations that align with your mission can provide access to capital, resources, and market reach. Seek out like-minded partners who can not only invest but also add value through their expertise, networks, and market presence.

Remember, each funding option comes with its own advantages and considerations. Tailor your approach to align with your venture's unique needs and financial goals. Developing a solid business plan, demonstrating traction, and showcasing your passion for sustainability will go a long way in attracting the right investors who share your vision for a better, more sustainable future.

As an entrepreneur, understanding these funding options and exploring them diligently will empower you to secure the necessary capital to bring your sustainable start-up to life and create a lasting impact in your chosen niche.

Crafting an Effective Pitch Deck

As an entrepreneur in the startup niche, one of the most crucial skills you need to master is the art of pitching your business idea effectively. A well-crafted pitch deck can make all the difference in securing funding, attracting potential investors, and ultimately launching a sustainable startup. In this subchapter, we will delve into the key elements and strategies for creating an impactful pitch deck that will leave a lasting impression on your audience.

First and foremost, your pitch deck should have a clear and concise structure. Begin with a compelling executive summary that highlights the problem your startup aims to solve and the unique solution you offer. This section should be concise yet captivating, grabbing the attention of potential investors from the very beginning.

Next, outline the market opportunity and target audience. Highlight the size and growth potential of the market, demonstrating that there is a demand for your product or service. By showcasing your understanding of the market landscape, you will build credibility and trust with your audience.

Following the market analysis, it's crucial to present your solution. Explain how your product or service addresses the identified problem and why it is superior to existing alternatives. Use visuals and examples to make your solution tangible and easier to grasp.

Another essential component of your pitch deck is the business model. Clearly define your revenue streams, pricing strategy, and how you plan to monetize your startup. This section should demonstrate the viability and profitability of your business model, instilling confidence in potential investors.

Furthermore, don't forget to include information about your team. Highlight the expertise and experience of your key team members, emphasizing their ability to execute the business plan effectively. Investors often invest in people as much as in ideas, so make sure to showcase the talent and dedication within your team.

Last but not least, end your pitch deck with a call to action. Clearly state what you are seeking from potential investors, whether it's funding, partnerships, or further discussions. Provide your contact information and be readily available to answer any questions or concerns.

Crafting an effective pitch deck is an ongoing process. Continuously refine and update your presentation as your startup evolves and grows. Remember, a well-crafted pitch deck can be the key to unlocking the support and resources necessary to turn your idea into a successful and sustainable startup.

Building Relationships with Impact Investors and Funders

In the world of sustainable start-ups, establishing strong relationships with impact investors and funders is crucial for success. These individuals and organizations not only provide the necessary financial support but also bring valuable expertise, networks, and credibility to the table. This subchapter aims to guide entrepreneurs in building meaningful connections with impact investors and funders, helping them secure the resources needed to launch and grow their start-ups.

1.   Understanding   Impact   Investors   and   Funders: Before reaching out to potential investors and funders, it is essential to understand their motivations and expectations. Impact investors are specifically interested in supporting ventures that generate positive social and environmental impact alongside financial returns. Funders, on the other hand, may include foundations, philanthropists, or government agencies focused on sustainability. By aligning your start-up's mission and values with these investors' objectives, you can increase your chances of building fruitful relationships.

2.   Research   and   Identify   Potential   Partners: Conduct thorough research to identify impact investors and funders who have previously supported similar ventures or have shown interest in your industry. Look for investors who align with your start-up's values and mission. Utilize online platforms, attend industry events, and network with other entrepreneurs to

find potential partners. Remember, building relationships is a long-term commitment, so choose your partners wisely.

3.   Craft   a   Compelling   Narrative: Develop a compelling narrative that clearly communicates your start-up's purpose, impact goals, and potential financial returns. Impact investors and funders want to understand the problem you are addressing and how your solution is unique and scalable. Craft a powerful story that can captivate their attention and resonate with their values.

4.   Build   Trust   and   Credibility: Investors and funders seek entrepreneurs who not only have a great idea but also possess the skills, determination, and integrity to execute it successfully. Establishing trust and credibility is crucial. Highlight relevant experience, expertise, and achievements that demonstrate your ability to deliver on your promises. Leverage your network to secure introductions and recommendations from trusted sources.

5.   Engage   in   Meaningful   Conversations: Once you have identified potential investors and funders, take the time to understand their interests and priorities. Engage in meaningful conversations to showcase how your start-up aligns with their goals. Seek their insights, advice, and feedback to build a mutually beneficial relationship. Remember, successful partnerships are built on open and transparent communication.

6.   Be   Prepared   for   Due   Diligence: When an investor or funder shows interest in your start-up, be

prepared for due diligence. This process involves a thorough examination of your business model, financial projections, team, and impact metrics. Ensure that your documentation and data are well-prepared, organized, and easily accessible.

Building relationships with impact investors and funders is a journey that requires patience, persistence, and perseverance. By understanding their motivations, crafting a compelling narrative, building trust, engaging in meaningful conversations, and being prepared for due diligence, entrepreneurs can position their start-ups for success in the sustainable start-up ecosystem.

Chapter 7: Developing a Sustainable Marketing Strategy

Creating a Brand Story around Sustainability

In today's business landscape, consumers are increasingly seeking out brands that align with their values and make a positive impact on the world. As an entrepreneur in the startup niche, it is crucial to recognize the growing importance of sustainability and to create a brand story that reflects your commitment to this cause. This subchapter will guide you through the process of creating a compelling brand story that resonates with your target audience and sets your startup apart from the competition.

First and foremost, it is essential to understand what sustainability means for your business. Are you focused on reducing carbon emissions, promoting ethical sourcing, or perhaps eliminating waste? By identifying your sustainability goals, you can begin crafting a brand story that showcases your unique mission and values. Remember, authenticity is key in gaining the trust and loyalty of your customers.

Once you have defined your sustainability goals, it's time to start weaving them into your brand story. Start by identifying the main message you want to convey. This could be centered around the positive impact your startup is making on the environment or society, or how your product or service promotes a more sustainable lifestyle. Whatever it may be, ensure that your message is clear, concise, and emotionally compelling.

Next, consider the various storytelling techniques you can employ to engage your audience. Storytelling is a powerful tool that can help create an emotional connection between your brand and your customers. Consider incorporating personal anecdotes, testimonials, or even visual elements such as videos or infographics to bring your brand story to life. Remember to highlight the unique aspects of your startup that make it truly sustainable and showcase the positive change you are bringing to the world.

Furthermore, leverage various marketing channels to amplify your brand story and reach a wider audience. Social media platforms, blogs, and press releases are all effective ways to communicate your sustainability initiatives and engage with your target market. Collaborate with influencers or partner with like-minded organizations to expand your reach and further strengthen your brand story.

Finally, consistently communicate your sustainability efforts and progress to your audience. Transparency is crucial in building trust and loyalty. Share updates on your achievements, challenges, and future goals. By being open and honest, you will not only foster a deeper connection with your customers but also inspire them to join you on your sustainability journey.

In conclusion, creating a brand story around sustainability is not only a powerful marketing strategy but also a way to differentiate your startup in the crowded marketplace. By defining your sustainability goals, crafting a compelling brand message, utilizing storytelling techniques, and consistently communicating your efforts, you can establish your startup as a leader in sustainability and attract customers who share your values. Embrace sustainability as a core aspect of your brand and showcase the positive impact you are making in the world.

Leveraging Digital Marketing for Sustainable Start-ups

In today's digital age, successfully launching and scaling a sustainable start-up requires more than just a great idea. Entrepreneurs must embrace the power of digital marketing to effectively reach and engage their target audience. This subchapter will delve into the various ways start-ups can leverage digital marketing strategies to maximize their impact and achieve long-term success.

One of the key advantages of digital marketing is its cost-effectiveness compared to traditional marketing channels. Start-ups often have limited resources, making it crucial to allocate their budget wisely. Digital marketing allows entrepreneurs to reach a wider audience at a fraction of the cost of traditional advertising methods. By leveraging social media platforms, search engine optimization (SEO), and content marketing, start-ups can create a strong online presence and drive organic traffic to their websites.

Furthermore, digital marketing provides start-ups with valuable data and analytics that can inform their decision-making process. By tracking website visitors, engagement rates, and conversion rates, entrepreneurs can gain insights into their target audience's preferences and behaviors. This data-driven approach enables start-ups to refine their marketing strategies, optimize their conversion funnels, and ultimately improve their overall business performance.

Social media platforms have become an integral part of our daily lives, and entrepreneurs must harness their potential to build brand awareness and foster a loyal customer base. By creating engaging content, interacting with followers, and running targeted advertising campaigns on platforms like Facebook, Instagram, and LinkedIn, start-ups can effectively reach their target audience and build meaningful connections.

Additionally, search engine optimization (SEO) plays a vital role in driving organic traffic to a start-up's website. By optimizing website content and structure, start-ups can improve their search engine rankings and increase their visibility to potential customers. Investing in SEO can lead to long-term benefits, as higher rankings equate to more organic traffic and potential sales.

Content marketing is another powerful tool for start-ups. By creating valuable and informative content, such as blog posts, videos, and infographics, entrepreneurs can establish themselves as industry experts and build trust with their audience. Sharing this content through various channels, including social media and email newsletters, can help start-ups attract and nurture leads, ultimately leading to increased conversions and sales.

In conclusion, digital marketing is an essential component of launching and scaling sustainable start-ups. By strategically leveraging social media, SEO, and content marketing, entrepreneurs can effectively reach their target audience, build brand awareness, and drive long-term success. Embracing digital marketing strategies will not only maximize a start-up's reach and impact but also ensure its sustainability in the competitive business landscape.

Engaging with Customers and Building a Community

In the competitive landscape of start-ups, engaging with customers and building a community around your brand is crucial for long-term success. As an entrepreneur, understanding the importance of customer interaction and fostering a strong sense of community should be at the forefront of your business strategy.

One of the first steps in engaging with customers is to truly understand their needs and desires. Conduct market research, gather feedback, and actively listen to your target audience. This will not only help you tailor your products or services to meet their expectations but also build a foundation of trust and loyalty.

Utilizing social media platforms is an effective way to connect with customers and build a community. Through platforms like Facebook, Instagram, and Twitter, you can directly engage with your audience, share valuable content, and address their concerns or queries. Regularly posting updates, conducting polls, and initiating discussions can create a sense of belonging and involvement among your customers.

Another powerful tool for customer engagement is hosting events or workshops. These events not only provide an opportunity for customers to interact with your brand but also enable them to network with like-minded individuals in your community. By organizing informative sessions or hands-on workshops related to your product or industry, you can establish your start-up as a thought leader and gain credibility.

Building a community goes beyond just customer engagement. It involves creating a space where customers feel valued and connected to one another. Consider creating an online forum or platform specifically for your customers to share their experiences, ask questions, and provide feedback. Encourage them to share their success stories and testimonials, which can serve as powerful marketing tools.

Collaboration is also key when building a community. Seek partnerships with complementary businesses or organizations to offer joint promotions or events. This not only expands your reach but also strengthens your brand's reputation by association.

Remember, building a community takes time and dedication. Consistency and authenticity are crucial. Be responsive to your customers' needs, address their concerns promptly, and consistently provide valuable content. By engaging with customers and building a community, you'll create a strong foundation for your start-up's success and foster a loyal customer base that will support your growth for years to come.

Chapter 8: Building Partnerships and Collaborations for Impact

Identifying Potential Partners and Collaborators

In the exciting journey of launching a sustainable start-up, one crucial aspect that entrepreneurs often overlook is the power of partnerships and collaborations. As an entrepreneur, it is essential to recognize that success does not solely rely on individual efforts but is also greatly influenced by the strength of your network and the ability to form strategic partnerships. This subchapter aims to guide entrepreneurs in identifying potential partners and collaborators, highlighting the immense benefits that can arise from such alliances.

The first step to identifying potential partners and collaborators is to clearly define your start-up's vision, goals, and values. Armed with this clarity, you can then seek out individuals and organizations that align with your purpose and can contribute to your venture's growth. Look for partners who possess complementary skills, expertise, and resources that can enhance your start-up's capabilities. Collaborating with like-minded individuals or organizations also reinforces your commitment to sustainability and amplifies your impact.

One effective way to identify potential partners is by attending industry conferences, trade shows, and networking events. These gatherings provide opportunities to meet and connect with individuals who share your passion for entrepreneurship and may be interested in collaborating. Engage in meaningful conversations, exchange ideas, and seek out individuals who can add value to your start-up. Additionally, online platforms and social media groups dedicated to start-ups and entrepreneurship can serve as valuable resources for building connections and finding potential partners.

Another avenue for identifying partners and collaborators is through conducting thorough market research. Analyze your industry's landscape, identify successful entrepreneurs or start-ups, and explore how their expertise can complement your own. Reach out to them with a well-crafted proposal highlighting the mutual benefits of collaboration. Emphasize how partnering with your start-up can create a win-win situation, such as expanding their market reach or enhancing their sustainability efforts.

Furthermore, consider forming alliances with non-profit organizations, government agencies, or academic institutions that align with your start-up's mission and values. These entities often possess extensive networks, resources, and knowledge that can prove invaluable in your entrepreneurial journey. Collaborating with such organizations not only provides access to a larger audience but can also enhance your credibility and open doors to funding opportunities.

In conclusion, identifying potential partners and collaborators is a crucial step for sustainable start-ups. By seeking out individuals and organizations that align with your vision and values, you can leverage their skills, expertise, and resources to amplify your impact. Attend relevant events, conduct market research, and explore collaborations with non-profit organizations or academic institutions to expand your network and increase your start-up's chances of success. Remember, partnerships and collaborations are key ingredients for transforming your idea into a thriving, sustainable venture.

Establishing Mutually Beneficial Relationships

In the highly competitive world of start-ups, establishing mutually beneficial relationships is crucial for long-term success. As an entrepreneur, you cannot underestimate the power of building strong connections with various stakeholders, including customers, suppliers, investors, and even competitors. This subchapter will delve into the importance of establishing these relationships, as well as provide practical tips for nurturing them.

One of the key benefits of cultivating mutually beneficial relationships is the opportunity for collaboration and knowledge sharing. By forming alliances with other start-ups or established companies in your niche, you can tap into their expertise, resources, and networks. Collaborative efforts often lead to innovative solutions and accelerated growth. For instance, partnering with a supplier who shares your commitment to sustainability can not only enhance your brand image but also create a win-win situation by reducing costs and environmental impact.

Another crucial aspect of establishing mutually beneficial relationships lies in understanding and meeting the needs of your customers. By actively listening to their feedback and engaging in open dialogue, you can build a loyal customer base and gain valuable insights for improving your product or service. Additionally, forging strong relationships with customers can lead to positive word-of-mouth referrals, which are often more effective than traditional marketing efforts.

When it comes to investors, building trust and credibility is essential. Establishing transparent and honest communication channels is crucial for attracting investors and securing funding. By keeping them informed about your progress, challenges, and long-term vision, you can establish a solid foundation for a mutually beneficial relationship. Moreover, investors often bring more than just financial support – their experience, industry connections, and strategic guidance can propel your start-up to new heights.

Lastly, it is important to recognize the potential benefits of building relationships with your competitors. While competition is fierce, there are often opportunities for collaboration and knowledge exchange. By establishing respectful relationships, you can learn from their successes and failures, identify potential partnerships, and even explore joint ventures that can benefit both parties.

In conclusion, establishing mutually beneficial relationships is a fundamental aspect of launching and sustaining a successful start-up. By nurturing connections with customers, suppliers, investors, and even competitors, you can tap into their expertise, resources, and networks, fostering collaboration and accelerating growth. Remember, in the world of entrepreneurship, building strong relationships is not only beneficial but also essential for long-term success.

Leveraging Collective Impact for Greater Change

In the world of entrepreneurship and start-ups, the potential for creating positive change is immense. As entrepreneurs, we have the unique opportunity to not only build successful businesses but also to address pressing social and environmental challenges. However, the magnitude of these challenges often requires collaboration and collective action to achieve meaningful and sustainable impact.

This subchapter explores the concept of leveraging collective impact for greater change and how it can be a game-changer for start-ups. Collective impact refers to the idea that large-scale social change can be achieved when organizations from different sectors work together towards a common goal. It recognizes that complex problems cannot be solved by a single entity alone, but rather through the power of collaboration and shared resources.

One of the key benefits of leveraging collective impact is the ability to pool expertise, resources, and networks. Start-ups often face limited resources and a lack of established networks, which can be significant barriers to success. By partnering with other organizations, entrepreneurs can tap into a wider range of expertise and leverage shared resources to accelerate their growth and impact.

Moreover, collective impact allows start-ups to amplify their influence and reach. By aligning with other like-minded organizations, entrepreneurs can create a unified voice that attracts attention and support from stakeholders, including investors, policymakers, and customers. This increased visibility not only opens doors to new opportunities but also helps in building credibility and trust.

Additionally, collective impact enables start-ups to tackle systemic issues that may be beyond their individual scope. Many social and environmental challenges are deeply rooted in complex systems, requiring multi-faceted approaches for effective solutions. By collaborating with diverse stakeholders, start-ups can address these systemic issues holistically, leading to more sustainable and long-lasting impact.

However, leveraging collective impact requires intentional and strategic efforts. Start-ups need to identify and engage with partners who share a common vision and values. Building strong relationships based on trust and mutual respect is vital for successful collaboration. Clear communication, defined roles and responsibilities, and a shared measurement system are also crucial to ensure alignment and track progress collectively.

In conclusion, leveraging collective impact is a powerful strategy for start-ups to achieve greater change. By collaborating with other organizations, entrepreneurs can tap into resources, amplify their influence, and address systemic challenges. As we embark on the journey of launching sustainable start-ups, let us embrace the power of collective action and work together to create a more inclusive, equitable, and sustainable future.

Chapter 9: Scaling and Measuring Impact

Strategies for Scaling Sustainable Start-ups

Scaling a sustainable start-up can be a challenging task, but with the right strategies in place, it is possible to achieve significant growth while staying true to your core values. In this subchapter, we will explore some effective strategies that can help entrepreneurs navigate the complexities of scaling their sustainable start-ups.

1. Build a Strong Foundation: Before even thinking about scaling, it is crucial to establish a solid foundation for your start-up. This includes a clear mission and vision, a strong team, and a well-defined value proposition. By having these elements in place, you will be better equipped to handle the challenges that come with growth.

2. Focus on Innovation: Sustainable start-ups thrive on innovation. Continuously seek ways to improve your products or services, and be open to feedback from customers and stakeholders. Innovation can help you differentiate your start-up from competitors and attract a larger customer base.

3. Collaborate and Partner: Collaboration can be a powerful tool for scaling sustainable start-ups. Look for opportunities to collaborate with other businesses, NGOs, or government organizations that share similar values and goals. By partnering with like-minded organizations, you can leverage their resources, expertise, and networks to accelerate your growth.

4. Embrace Technology: Technology can play a crucial role in scaling sustainable start-ups. Explore how you can leverage digital platforms, automation, and data analytics to streamline your operations, enhance customer experiences, and improve efficiency. Technology can help you reach a wider audience and expand your market reach.

5. Access Funding and Resources: Scaling requires adequate funding and resources. Seek out investors, venture capitalists, and grants that align with your sustainable mission. Additionally, consider joining accelerators or incubators that provide mentorship, networking opportunities, and access to a community of like-minded entrepreneurs.

6. Develop a Scalable Business Model: A scalable business model is essential for sustainable start-ups aiming to grow rapidly. Assess your current business model and identify areas where scalability can be improved. This may involve refining your pricing structure, exploring new distribution channels, or diversifying revenue streams.

7. Prioritize Talent Acquisition and Retention: As your start-up scales, attracting and retaining top talent becomes crucial. Hiring individuals who are passionate about your mission and possess the necessary skills can contribute significantly to your growth. Additionally, invest in employee development programs and create a positive work culture to ensure talent retention.

Scaling a sustainable start-up requires careful planning, strategic thinking, and a commitment to your mission. By implementing these strategies, entrepreneurs in the start-up niche can navigate the challenges of growth while remaining true to their sustainable values, ultimately driving long-term impact and success.

Implementing Impact Measurement and Reporting

As a start-up entrepreneur, one of the key aspects of running a sustainable business is measuring and reporting the impact your venture has on the environment, society, and the economy. By implementing effective impact measurement and reporting strategies, you not only gain a deeper understanding of your business's effects but also demonstrate your commitment to transparency and responsible practices. This subchapter will guide you through the process of implementing impact measurement and reporting in your start-up.

1. Define your impact goals: Start by clearly identifying the social and environmental issues your start-up aims to address. Determine the specific outcomes you want to achieve, whether it's reducing carbon emissions, promoting gender equality, or supporting local communities. These impact goals will serve as a framework for your measurement and reporting efforts.

2. Identify key performance indicators (KPIs): Once you have defined your impact goals, identify the KPIs that will help you track progress towards those goals. For example, if your goal is to reduce carbon emissions, relevant KPIs may include energy consumption, waste production, or emissions per unit of production. Ensure that your KPIs align with the United Nations Sustainable Development Goals (SDGs) to provide a standardized framework for measurement.

3. Collect and analyze data: Establish a system for collecting relevant data to measure your KPIs. This might involve

integrating technology to capture real-time data or partnering with external organizations for data collaboration. Regularly analyze this data to assess your performance against your impact goals and identify areas for improvement.

4. Develop impact reports: Use the data collected to create impact reports that communicate the progress and outcomes of your start-up's initiatives. These reports should be clear, concise, and easily understandable to various stakeholders, including investors, customers, and employees. Include both quantitative data and qualitative stories to provide a holistic view of your impact.

5. Engage stakeholders: Involve your stakeholders throughout the impact measurement and reporting process. Seek feedback and input from your customers, employees, and community members to enhance the accuracy and reliability of your impact reports. This engagement will also foster trust and credibility among your stakeholders.

6. Continuous improvement: Impact measurement and reporting is an ongoing process. Regularly review and refine your impact goals, KPIs, and data collection methods to ensure they remain relevant and meaningful. Stay updated on industry best practices and emerging standards to enhance the effectiveness and credibility of your impact measurement efforts.

By implementing robust impact measurement and reporting practices, your start-up can not only drive positive change but also attract investors, customers, and talent who align with your values. Use this subchapter as a guide to embed impact measurement and reporting into the core of your sustainable start-up.

Overcoming Challenges in Scaling Sustainability

Scaling sustainability is a significant challenge faced by many start-ups aiming to make a positive impact on the world. While launching a sustainable start-up is a commendable feat, ensuring its long-term viability and scalability is a complex task. In this subchapter, we will explore the various challenges entrepreneurs encounter when scaling sustainability and provide actionable strategies to overcome them.

One of the primary challenges in scaling sustainability is the availability of resources. As start-ups grow, they require additional funding, talented human resources, and technological infrastructure to expand their operations. However, securing funding for sustainable initiatives can be challenging, as investors may perceive them as high-risk or lacking profitability. Entrepreneurs must proactively seek out impact-focused investors and explore alternative financing options, such as grants, crowdfunding, or partnerships with like-minded organizations.

Another key challenge lies in ensuring the scalability of sustainable practices. Start-ups often face difficulties in replicating their sustainable models as they expand geographically or enter new markets. Local regulations, cultural differences, and limited access to sustainable resources can pose obstacles. Entrepreneurs must adapt their business models to suit different contexts while maintaining their core sustainability principles. Collaborating with local stakeholders, conducting rigorous market research, and engaging in continuous learning are crucial strategies to overcome these challenges.

Additionally, integrating sustainable practices into the supply chain can be a formidable hurdle for scaling sustainability. Start-ups may face difficulties finding suppliers who share their commitment to sustainability and ethical practices. To overcome this challenge, entrepreneurs should actively seek out and collaborate with suppliers who align with their values. Building long-term relationships with suppliers and providing them with incentives for adopting sustainable practices can create a virtuous cycle of positive impact throughout the supply chain.

Lastly, scaling sustainability requires effective communication and building a strong brand reputation. Start-ups must convey their sustainability initiatives and impact to consumers, investors, and other stakeholders. Entrepreneurs should develop clear and compelling messaging that highlights the unique value proposition of their sustainable start-up. Leveraging digital platforms, social media, and partnerships with influencers can help raise awareness and build a loyal customer base.

In conclusion, scaling sustainability is a multifaceted challenge for start-ups. Entrepreneurs must navigate the hurdles of securing resources, adapting business models, integrating sustainability into the supply chain, and effectively communicating their impact. By implementing the strategies outlined in this subchapter, sustainable start-ups can overcome these challenges and maximize their potential for creating a lasting positive impact on the world.

Chapter 10: Navigating Legal and Regulatory Challenges

Understanding Environmental and Social Regulations

As an entrepreneur in the start-up world, it is essential to have a solid understanding of environmental and social regulations. In today's society, consumers are increasingly conscious of the impact businesses have on the environment and society at large. By familiarizing yourself with these regulations, you can ensure that your start-up not only complies with legal requirements but also contributes positively to the world.

Environmental regulations are laws put in place to protect the environment and promote sustainable practices. These regulations cover a wide range of areas, including waste management, air and water pollution, energy efficiency, and carbon emissions. By adhering to these regulations, you can minimize the negative environmental impact of your start-up and potentially access various incentives and grants that encourage sustainable practices.

Social regulations, on the other hand, focus on issues related to social responsibility and human rights. These regulations aim to ensure fair treatment of employees, prevent discrimination, promote diversity and inclusion, and protect consumer rights. By complying with social regulations, you can create a positive work environment, build a strong brand reputation, and attract socially conscious consumers.

To navigate environmental and social regulations effectively, it is crucial to stay updated on any changes or new developments. Regulatory bodies often revise and update regulations to adapt to emerging challenges and societal needs. This information can be obtained from government websites, industry associations, or by consulting legal professionals with expertise in environmental and social law.

Engaging in proactive compliance measures is also essential. Conducting regular audits to assess your start-up's environmental and social practices can help identify areas for improvement and ensure ongoing compliance. Implementing robust reporting and monitoring systems enables you to track your progress and demonstrate transparency to stakeholders.

Furthermore, understanding the potential benefits of compliance is vital. By adhering to environmental and social regulations, your start-up can gain a competitive advantage. Consumers are increasingly favoring businesses that demonstrate a commitment to sustainability and social responsibility. Compliance can also open doors to partnerships and collaborations with like-minded organizations and investors who prioritize ethical practices.

In conclusion, as an entrepreneur in the start-up space, understanding environmental and social regulations is of utmost importance. By complying with these regulations, you can not only avoid legal repercussions but also position your start-up as a force for positive change. Embracing sustainability and social responsibility will not only benefit the planet and society but also contribute to the long-term success and resilience of your business.

Ensuring Compliance and Risk Management

In the fast-paced world of start-ups, entrepreneurs often find themselves caught up in the whirlwind of developing innovative ideas, securing funding, and building a strong team. While these aspects are crucial for the success of any start-up, it is equally important to prioritize compliance and risk management.

Compliance refers to adhering to legal and regulatory requirements specific to your industry. Failure to comply with these regulations can have serious consequences, including legal penalties and reputational damage. Risk management, on the other hand, involves identifying and mitigating potential risks that could impact the business's operations, finances, or reputation.

To ensure compliance and effective risk management, entrepreneurs must adopt a proactive approach. Here are some key considerations to keep in mind:

1. Understand the regulatory landscape: Familiarize yourself with all relevant laws and regulations that govern your industry. Seek legal counsel if needed to ensure full compliance. This includes areas such as data protection, employment, intellectual property, and consumer rights.

2. Develop internal policies and procedures: Establish clear guidelines and protocols for your start-up. These should outline how the company will adhere to legal requirements, manage risks, and promote ethical practices. Regularly review and update these policies to reflect changes in laws or industry best practices.

3. Implement robust data protection measures: In today's digital age, data protection is a critical aspect of compliance. Safeguarding customer and employee data is not only a legal requirement but also crucial for maintaining trust with stakeholders. Invest in secure systems, educate your team on data privacy, and implement appropriate measures to prevent data breaches.

4. Conduct regular risk assessments: Identify potential risks that could hinder your start-up's growth or disrupt operations. This could include financial risks, cybersecurity threats, supply chain vulnerabilities, or even reputational risks. Regularly assess and prioritize these risks, and develop strategies to mitigate them.

5. Foster a culture of compliance: Compliance and risk management should be ingrained in your start-up's culture. Educate your team about the importance of compliance and their individual responsibilities. Encourage open communication and reporting of any potential compliance issues or risks.

By prioritizing compliance and risk management, entrepreneurs can safeguard their start-ups, build trust with stakeholders, and position themselves as responsible businesses. This not only protects their interests but also opens doors to new opportunities and partnerships. Remember, compliance and risk management are ongoing processes, requiring continuous monitoring and adaptation to ensure the long-term success of your start-up.

Advocating for Policy Changes and Industry Standards

In the dynamic world of start-ups, entrepreneurs often find themselves at the forefront of innovation, challenging the status quo and striving to make a lasting impact on society. As a start-up founder, it is not only important to focus on building a successful business but also to advocate for policy changes and industry standards that align with your sustainable goals. This subchapter aims to guide entrepreneurs on how to effectively advocate for these changes and create a positive impact within their industries.

One of the first steps in advocating for policy changes is to understand the current landscape and identify areas where improvements can be made. Conduct thorough research on existing policies and regulations that directly impact your start-up's operations. This knowledge will help you identify gaps and inconsistencies that need to be addressed. Additionally, stay updated with industry trends and best practices to ensure that your advocacy efforts are relevant and impactful.

Once you have identified the areas where policy changes are needed, it is crucial to build a coalition of like-minded individuals and organizations. Collaborate with other start-ups, industry associations, and non-profit organizations that share your goals. By joining forces, you can amplify your message and increase your chances of success. Together, you can lobby policymakers, organize events, and draft policy proposals that advocate for sustainable practices and support the growth of start-ups in your industry.

Effective communication is key when advocating for policy changes and industry standards. Craft a compelling narrative that highlights the positive impact that your proposed changes will have on both the environment and the economy. Use data, case studies, and real-life examples to back up your claims. Furthermore, leverage various communication channels such as social media, industry conferences, and mainstream media to raise awareness about your cause. Engage with key stakeholders, policymakers, and influencers to foster productive conversations and gain support for your initiatives.

Remember that advocating for policy changes and industry standards is a long-term commitment. It requires persistence, resilience, and a willingness to adapt your strategies along the way. Celebrate small victories and learn from setbacks to refine your approach. By actively participating in shaping policies and standards, entrepreneurs can contribute to a more sustainable and thriving start-up ecosystem.

In conclusion, advocating for policy changes and industry standards is a crucial aspect of launching a sustainable start-up. By understanding the current landscape, building coalitions, communicating effectively, and engaging with stakeholders, entrepreneurs can drive meaningful change within their industries. Embrace the opportunity to advocate for a better future, and let your start-up become a catalyst for positive transformation.

Chapter 11: Case Studies of Successful Sustainable Start-ups

Real-Life Examples of Sustainable Start-ups

As an entrepreneur venturing into the start-up world, it is important to have role models and real-life examples to draw inspiration and guidance from. This subchapter, "Real-Life Examples of Sustainable Start-ups," aims to provide you with a glimpse into the success stories of sustainable start-ups in various niches. These examples serve as a testament to the fact that sustainable practices and profitability can go hand in hand.

1. Patagonia: Founded by Yvon Chouinard, Patagonia is a clothing company that has become a global leader in sustainability. They prioritize using recycled and organic materials, reducing waste, and promoting fair labor practices. Patagonia's commitment to sustainability has not only attracted environmentally conscious customers but has also resulted in significant growth and profitability.

2. Beyond Meat: This plant-based meat substitute company has revolutionized the food industry. By creating products that mimic the taste and texture of real meat, Beyond Meat has attracted both vegetarians and meat-eaters concerned about the environmental impact of animal agriculture. Their sustainable business model has garnered immense popularity, leading to partnerships with major fast-food chains and substantial financial success.

3. Tesla: Elon Musk's electric car company, Tesla, has disrupted the automotive industry by offering environmentally friendly alternatives to traditional vehicles. Tesla's commitment to reducing carbon emissions and dependence on fossil fuels has not only resonated with eco-conscious consumers but has also proven to be a lucrative business strategy. The company's market capitalization has soared, making it one of the most valuable car manufacturers globally.

4. TOMS: Known for their "One for One" model, TOMS is a shoe company that donates a pair of shoes to a child in need for every pair purchased. This simple yet impactful approach to corporate social responsibility has resonated with consumers, leading to TOMS' rapid growth and expansion into other product categories. Their success is a testament to the power of aligning business goals with social impact.

These real-life examples demonstrate that sustainable start-ups can thrive in various industries, appealing to consumers who prioritize ethical and environmentally friendly products. By incorporating sustainable practices into your business model, you not only contribute to a greener future but also open doors to new market opportunities and financial success. As you embark on your entrepreneurial journey, take inspiration from these success stories and strive to make a positive impact through your own sustainable start-up.

Lessons Learned from Their Journey to Impact

In the ever-evolving world of entrepreneurship, the journey from idea to impact is filled with challenges, setbacks, and triumphs. Successful start-ups have paved the way for aspiring entrepreneurs, offering valuable lessons that can guide and inspire others on their own path to making a sustainable impact.

1. Embrace Failure as a Stepping Stone: One common thread among successful start-ups is their ability to learn from failure. Embrace setbacks as learning opportunities, as they often provide invaluable insights that can lead to breakthroughs. Remember, failure is not final; it is merely a detour on the road to success.

2. Seek Out Mentorship: No entrepreneur can navigate the start-up landscape alone. Seek guidance from experienced mentors who have already walked a similar path. Their wisdom and perspective can help you avoid common pitfalls and provide valuable insights that can accelerate your journey.

3. Build a Strong Team: Your team is the backbone of your start-up. Surround yourself with individuals who share your vision, complement your skills, and bring diverse perspectives to the table. A cohesive and motivated team is essential for overcoming challenges and driving sustainable growth.

4. Be Agile and Adapt: The start-up landscape is constantly changing, and agility is key to survival. Be open to pivoting your business model, adjusting your strategies, and embracing new technologies. Adapting to market demands and evolving consumer needs is crucial for long-term success.

5. Focus on Customer Insights: Your customers hold the key to unlocking your start-up's potential impact. Listen to their feedback, understand their pain points, and continuously iterate your product or service to exceed their expectations. By putting customer insights at the forefront, you can build a loyal customer base and drive sustainable growth.

6. Embrace Sustainability: In today's world, sustainability is no longer a niche; it's a necessity. Incorporate sustainable practices into your start-up's DNA from the very beginning. Consider the environmental, social, and economic impacts of your business decisions, and strive to create a positive change in the world.

7. Stay Resilient: The road to impact is rarely smooth. There will be times when you feel overwhelmed, discouraged, or even on the verge of giving up. Stay resilient, persevere through challenges, and maintain a strong belief in your mission. It is during these moments that true entrepreneurs rise above, bringing their ideas to life and making a lasting impact.

In "From Idea to Impact: A Guide to Launching Sustainable Start-ups," these lessons learned from successful entrepreneurs serve as a roadmap for aspiring entrepreneurs. By embracing failure, seeking mentorship, building strong teams, adapting to change, focusing on customer insights, embracing sustainability, and staying resilient, entrepreneurs can navigate the start-up landscape and launch ventures that make a meaningful and lasting impact.

Insights and Inspiration from Sustainable Entrepreneurs

Subchapter: Insights and Inspiration from Sustainable Entrepreneurs

Introduction:

In this subchapter, we delve into the invaluable insights and inspiration shared by successful sustainable entrepreneurs. Their experiences, challenges, and triumphs offer a wealth of knowledge for aspiring entrepreneurs in the startup niche. Drawing from their stories, we aim to motivate and guide you on your own sustainable startup journey.

Harnessing Passion and Purpose: Sustainable entrepreneurs often have a burning passion and a strong sense of purpose in their endeavors. They believe that their startups can make a positive impact on society and the environment. Through interviews and case studies, we explore how these entrepreneurs discovered their passion and how they align it with their business goals. By understanding their mindset, you can develop your own sense of purpose and drive to create a sustainable startup that truly makes a difference.

Overcoming Challenges: Starting a sustainable business can be an uphill battle, with numerous challenges along the way. From securing funding to navigating complex regulations, sustainable entrepreneurs face unique obstacles. We share stories of entrepreneurs who successfully overcame these challenges, providing practical advice and strategies for you to apply to your own startup. Learn how they turned setbacks into opportunities, and gain insights into effective problem-solving techniques.

Innovative Solutions for a Better Future: One of the hallmarks of sustainable entrepreneurs is their ability to think outside the box and develop innovative solutions to pressing global issues. We highlight groundbreaking ideas and products that have emerged from the sustainable startup ecosystem. These range from renewable energy technologies to creative approaches to waste management and ethical sourcing. By exploring these innovations, you can gain inspiration for your own startup and discover new possibilities for addressing sustainability challenges.

Building a Supportive Ecosystem: Sustainable entrepreneurs emphasize the importance of collaboration and building a supportive ecosystem. We explore how these entrepreneurs leveraged networks, partnerships, and mentorship to accelerate their startup's growth. Discover the resources available to you, such as sustainable incubators, accelerators, and funding opportunities. Learn from their experiences to cultivate a strong support network for your own venture.

Conclusion:

Insights and inspiration from sustainable entrepreneurs offer invaluable guidance for aspiring entrepreneurs in the startup niche. By harnessing passion and purpose, overcoming challenges, developing innovative solutions, and building a supportive ecosystem, you can launch a sustainable startup that creates a positive impact. The stories shared in this subchapter demonstrate that sustainable entrepreneurship is not only a viable path but also a rewarding journey towards a better future.

Chapter 12: The Future of Sustainable Start-ups

Emerging Trends and Opportunities

In the fast-paced world of entrepreneurship and start-ups, it is crucial to stay ahead of the curve and be aware of the emerging trends and opportunities that can propel your sustainable start-up to success. The landscape of business is constantly evolving, and as an entrepreneur, it is vital to adapt and seize the opportunities that arise. This subchapter explores some of the key emerging trends and opportunities that can shape the future of your start-up.

1. AI and Automation: Artificial Intelligence (AI) and automation technologies are revolutionizing various industries. From chatbots and virtual assistants to predictive analytics and machine learning algorithms, incorporating AI into your start-up can streamline processes, enhance customer experiences, and optimize resource allocation.

2. Sustainable Solutions: In recent years, there has been a significant shift towards sustainability and conscious consumerism. Entrepreneurs have a unique opportunity to develop products or services that address environmental challenges, such as renewable energy, waste reduction, and eco-friendly manufacturing processes. By aligning your start-up with sustainable practices, you can attract a growing base of environmentally conscious customers.

3. Digital Transformation: The digital revolution has disrupted traditional business models, and embracing digital transformation is crucial for start-ups. This includes leveraging cloud computing, data analytics, mobile technologies, and the Internet of Things (IoT) to improve efficiency, expand market reach, and enhance customer engagement.

4. Health and Wellness: The health and wellness industry has experienced significant growth in recent years, with consumers prioritizing physical and mental well-being. Entrepreneurs can tap into this market by developing innovative solutions, such as fitness apps, personalized nutrition plans, mental health platforms, and stress management tools.

5. E-commerce and Online Marketplaces: The rise of e-commerce and online marketplaces has revolutionized the way consumers shop. As an entrepreneur, you can leverage these platforms to reach a wider audience, reduce operational costs, and provide convenience to your customers. Building an online presence and optimizing your digital marketing strategies are crucial to tap into this growing trend.

6. Social Impact and Corporate Responsibility: Consumers are increasingly demanding that businesses contribute positively to society. Start-ups have the opportunity to integrate social impact into their business models, whether through sustainable sourcing, ethical manufacturing, or supporting social causes. By aligning your start-up with a purpose-driven mission, you can attract socially conscious customers and investors.

In conclusion, being aware of emerging trends and opportunities is vital for entrepreneurs and start-ups. Incorporating AI and automation, focusing on sustainability, embracing digital transformation, tapping into the health and wellness industry, leveraging e-commerce, and emphasizing social impact can lead to long-term success. By staying ahead of the curve and adapting to these trends, your start-up can make a significant impact in the market and thrive in the ever-evolving business landscape.

Innovations Driving Sustainable Entrepreneurship

In today's rapidly changing world, entrepreneurs and start-ups face numerous challenges. However, they also have unprecedented opportunities to make a positive impact on society and the environment. This subchapter explores the innovations that are driving sustainable entrepreneurship, providing insights and inspiration for aspiring and existing entrepreneurs.

One of the key innovations driving sustainable entrepreneurship is the advancement in renewable energy technologies. As the world grapples with the urgent need to transition from fossil fuels to clean energy sources, entrepreneurs are at the forefront of developing innovative solutions. From solar and wind power to biofuels and geothermal energy, start-ups are revolutionizing the way we produce and consume energy.

Another crucial innovation lies in the realm of sustainable materials and manufacturing. Entrepreneurs are exploring alternative materials that are not only environmentally friendly but also offer improved performance and durability. From biodegradable packaging to zero-waste manufacturing processes, start-ups are reimagining traditional supply chains and creating sustainable products that appeal to environmentally conscious consumers.

The digital revolution has also opened up new avenues for sustainable entrepreneurship. Tech entrepreneurs are leveraging the power of data, artificial intelligence, and blockchain to address pressing sustainability challenges. From smart grids and energy management systems to supply chain transparency and circular economy platforms, start-ups are harnessing the potential of digital technologies to create more efficient and sustainable systems.

Furthermore, social entrepreneurship is gaining momentum as a powerful force for positive change. Start-ups with a mission to address social and environmental issues are not only generating profits but also making a meaningful impact. By combining business acumen with social responsibility, these entrepreneurs are demonstrating that financial success and sustainability can go hand in hand.

Lastly, the concept of shared economy and collaborative consumption is transforming industries and paving the way for sustainable entrepreneurship. Start-ups are disrupting traditional business models by enabling resource sharing, reducing waste, and promoting a more efficient use of assets. From ride-sharing platforms to co-working spaces and community-driven initiatives, entrepreneurs are redefining how we consume and utilize resources.

In conclusion, innovations in renewable energy, sustainable materials, digital technologies, social entrepreneurship, and the shared economy are driving sustainable entrepreneurship. Entrepreneurs have an unprecedented opportunity to create businesses that not only generate profits but also contribute to a more sustainable and equitable future. By embracing these innovations, start-ups can make a lasting impact and inspire others to follow suit.

The Role of Sustainable Start-ups in Shaping a Better Future

In recent years, the world has witnessed a growing awareness and concern for environmental and social issues. As entrepreneurs, we have a unique opportunity to make a significant impact on the world around us through sustainable start-ups. This subchapter explores the crucial role that sustainable start-ups play in shaping a better future for our planet and society.

Sustainable start-ups are businesses that prioritize environmental and social responsibility alongside profitability. They are driven by the vision of creating positive change and are committed to finding innovative solutions to the pressing challenges we face. These start-ups are not only disrupting traditional industries but also revolutionizing the way business is conducted.

One of the key roles of sustainable start-ups is to drive the transition towards a greener economy. By developing and implementing sustainable practices, they reduce the carbon footprint and conserve natural resources. These start-ups are pioneers in renewable energy, circular economy, waste reduction, and eco-friendly products and services. Through their innovation and commitment to sustainability, they inspire and influence other businesses to adopt more responsible practices.

In addition to environmental impact, sustainable start-ups also address social issues. They prioritize fair labor practices, diversity and inclusion, and community engagement. By creating job opportunities, empowering marginalized communities, and supporting local economies, these start-ups contribute to inclusive growth and social equality.

Sustainable start-ups also serve as catalysts for change in established industries. They challenge the status quo by demonstrating that profitability and sustainability can go hand in hand. By proving the viability of sustainable business models, they encourage existing companies to rethink their strategies and embrace more responsible practices. This ripple effect spreads throughout the business ecosystem, creating a positive domino effect of change.

Furthermore, sustainable start-ups foster collaboration and knowledge sharing among entrepreneurs. They create networks and platforms where like-minded individuals can connect, exchange ideas, and collaborate on projects with shared goals. This collaborative approach not only accelerates innovation but also amplifies the impact of these start-ups.

In conclusion, sustainable start-ups play a pivotal role in shaping a better future for our planet and society. Through their innovative solutions, commitment to sustainability, and ability to disrupt established industries, they drive the transition towards a greener and more socially responsible economy. As entrepreneurs, we have the power to make a difference. By launching sustainable start-ups, we can contribute to a brighter future and inspire others to follow suit.

Conclusion: Taking Action and Making a Difference

Congratulations, entrepreneurs! You have embarked on an incredible journey by diving into the world of start-ups and sustainable entrepreneurship. Throughout this book, we have explored the process of transforming an idea into a tangible impact. Now, it is time to conclude our journey by emphasizing the significance of taking action and making a difference.

In the fast-paced world of start-ups, it is crucial to remember that ideas alone are not enough. It is the execution of these ideas that truly matters. As entrepreneurs, you have the power to bring about positive change in society, and this can only be achieved by taking action. The road ahead may be challenging, filled with obstacles and setbacks, but it is important to stay resilient and persevere.

One of the key elements of successful start-ups is the ability to make a difference. As you launch your sustainable start-up, always keep in mind the impact you aspire to create. Whether it is addressing social or environmental issues, your business should contribute towards a better future. By aligning your values with your business goals, you can create a powerful force for positive change.

Moreover, taking action also entails being adaptable and open to learning. The start-up landscape is ever-evolving, and it is essential to stay updated with the latest trends and innovations. Embrace feedback and continuously refine your strategies to ensure that you are making the greatest possible impact.

Collaboration with like-minded individuals and organizations can amplify your efforts, enabling you to reach a wider audience and achieve greater change.

Remember, making a difference is not limited to the direct impact of your start-up. It also involves inspiring others to follow suit and adopt sustainable practices. As entrepreneurs, you are not only leading by example but also empowering others to take action. Share your journey, successes, and challenges with the wider community, and encourage others to join the movement towards a more sustainable future.

In conclusion, the path from idea to impact is not an easy one, but it is a journey that is incredibly rewarding. By taking action and making a difference, you have the power to shape a better world through your start-up. Embrace the challenges, stay focused on your goals, and never lose sight of the positive change you aim to bring about. Together, let us revolutionize the start-up landscape and create a sustainable future for generations to come.